Author:
Jayme Carbaugh

Jayme is a self published author, she loves to bring stories alive with personal experiences through her work. Jayme has been in special education since 2010. She started as a Paraprofessional and has progressed her education to include teaching license and behavioral specialist.

Currently, working in the public school in Arizona. She is a wife, and a mother of 4. Hope you enjoy the book as much as she had fun creating it.

Illustrator:
Ashley Rangel

Ashley is an 18 year old artist with a passion for bringing stories to life through her artwork. From painting to graphic design, Ashley loves creating all forms of art.

Ashley's debut as a children's book illustrator came with "Ditty Kitty and the Wild Raccoons", where she ventured into the digital art world. Shifting in her artistic practice allowed her to blend traditional studio skills with modern digital techniques.

This is a story about a boy that lives in an imaginary world, learning how to make it in a world using his coping skills toolbox. He moves states and has to learn how to overcome challenges in a new school, with new friends and his ability to fit in. His alter ego Millie appears just in time to support him in situations that are challenging for a young child with Autism.

How will Millie help Lando Commando get through his first day at a new school?

This book is dedicated to my children, one whom is living his life dealing with Sensory Processing Disorder, ADHD and Apraxia. Also, to all the wonderful students I have had the honor of working with. There is a great life out there for you to embrace, and remember I will always be in your corner cheering for you!

"Bye Ohio!" Lando Commando sighed getting into the big moving truck while his friends stood in the yard waving "Bye, Lando!" They said together. "We will miss all our crazy adventures!"

Then just like that they were off to travel from Ohio to Arizona. Lando Commando looked in the truck side mirror and a single tear rolled down his cheek. He was unsure of what was to come from everything he knew as normal.

5

The struggle in a new state, is a new house, new friends and a new school. Lando Commando was feeling nervous, because new schools can be very scary.

The bus rolled up on the first day of school, all the kids were excited, smiling and got right onto the bus. Lando Commando froze, and could feel his heart beating, as if it were going to jump out of his chest.

"Let's go young man!" Yelled the bus driver. Lando took a final deep breath and got onto the bus.

As Lando was walking down the bus aisle one kid moved his book bag so Lando could not sit down.

Gabriel, a big 5th grader said, "Not here four eyes!" He felt defeated and looked at the ground but kept walking towards the back of the bus.

A little voice said to him "You can sit here if you want!" Lando smiled and sat down. He was relieved to have a seat and the kids stopped staring at him, he was the new kid after all.

During the first couple hours on his first day, Lando Commando could not focus. The room was very colorful and distracting, his teacher's voice was too loud, his desk buddy was tapping his pencil loud and fast on the desk, the fan was humming above him, and the ticking of the clock was making it hard for him to learn.

He put his head down on his desk and let out
a big sigh, he felt so overwhelmed.

His teacher came by, "What's wrong buddy?" "Ohhhh, my brain isn't letting me listen today!" He said in a sad tone. "Well?" said his teacher "I have something that may help you."

She got up and brought him a new seat and this seat was not like the others. This seat wiggles and made Lando Commando feel calm. He smiled looking at his teacher, "This is amazzzzzing! Thank you!" Millie smiled at Lando and twirled on her wiggle seat too.

At recess no one picked Lando Commando for the soccer team. He didn't get a turn on the swings. Third grade wasn't turning out to be fun at all.

He decided to sit on the bench, as he was walking, he heard the little voice again "You can play with me Lando Commando!" "REALLY?" Squealed Lando Commando.

"I know what it feels like when no one wants to play with you. I will be your friend. I am Millie and I have what my mom calls, Autism so I'm looked at differently." Said Millie with a smile on her face.

"Me too, but why did you smile?" He asked. "Because I'm happy being me and helping others make friends." She explained. " I am not scared to ask for things that make it easier for me to get through my day." She explained to Lando.

The same day, at lunch Millie asked Lando
Commando to sit with her, he gladly
accepted the invitation. "What is it like
wearing a cape to school, Lando? "I think
that is super cool." Millie said.

"Well, I..I..I wear it everyday. Ever since I was little, I can't go anywhere without it." Lando Commando told Millie. "I know my mother would like me to try and leave it at home while I was at school, I am just not ready." He told Millie. "It makes me feel safe."

"Can I try it on?" Asked Millie. "NO!" Lando yelled quickly. His heart started beating fast and a slight anger feeling came over him at the thought of her wearing his cape.

"Ohhhhh!" Millie said shyly. "I thought we were friends Lando Commando." Lando heard her say friends and his heartbeat slowed down and he looked at her... "W..w...we.. are?" He asked timidly. "YES!" She said excitedly.

Lando thought long and hard about her wearing his cape. What if she tore it, or didn't give it back? Millie stared at him patiently waiting on the cape.

He slowly removed the cape and handed it to her. "There! Now be careful Millie!" Lando demanded. He looked very nervous she had his cape on.

"Ok, give it back NOW. I don't like it when people touch my stuff!" He said to Millie. She gave it back and thanked him for being a good friend.

As the school day was coming to an end,
Lando Commando thought about how he can
make more friends tomorrow and he too can
be brave like Millie, he admired her for that.

It was time to get on the bus and this time
he was not afraid. Lando sat with Millie and
they talked about collection cards, games
they like and foods they would not eat
because they feel funny in their mouth.

He realized there are people out there just like him and it was a good day even if Millie was the only one that wanted to play with him. He was excited to see her tomorrow.

Walking in the door of his new house, Lando
Commando could not wait to take his shoes
off, they bothered him all day but he knew he
had to keep his shoes on at school.

Lando's mother came around the corner from the kitchen. "Lando Commando... I have your after school snack ready, cheesy-extra-cheesy crackers just like you have everyday."

He ran into the kitchen and told his Mother everything about his day; his nerves, the kids not picking him for games, the best part his friend Millie. "Ma! Millie and I are going to have great adventures, I just know it!"

"That is wonderful, Lando!" his mother said. "Yes, we are going to be best friends and maybe other people will see how happy we are and want to be our friends too!" Lando hopped off the table, twirled in his cape and darted off into the next room as if he were a superhero.

Lando's mom chuckled to herself, smiled as he ran off. "Oh, Lando I can't wait to see where all your abilities and adventures take you." She stated under her breath. The best is yet to come for you Lando Commando.